Great Wall of China

Carla Mooney

Rourke
Educational Media

rourkeeducationalmedia.com

Scan for Related Titles
and Teacher Resources

Before Reading:

Building Academic Vocabulary and Background Knowledge

Before reading a book, it is important to tap into what your child or students already know about the topic. This will help them develop their vocabulary, increase their reading comprehension, and make connections across the curriculum.

1. *Look at the cover of the book. What will this book be about?*
2. *What do you already know about the topic?*
3. *Let's study the Table of Contents. What will you learn about in the book's chapters?*
4. *What would you like to learn about this topic? Do you think you might learn about it from this book? Why or why not?*
5. *Use a reading journal to write about your knowledge of this topic. Record what you already know about the topic and what you hope to learn about the topic.*
6. *Read the book.*
7. *In your reading journal, record what you learned about the topic and your response to the book.*
8. *After reading the book complete the activities below.*

Content Area Vocabulary
Read the list. What do these words mean?

barbarians
brims
dynasty
emperor
fortifications
foundation
frontier
garrison
kilns
nomadic
provinces
raided
reeds
relics

After Reading:

Comprehension and Extension Activity

After reading the book, work on the following questions with your child or students in order to check their level of reading comprehension and content mastery.

1. *How did the purpose of the wall evolve over time? (Summarize)*
2. *Why is the wall in northern China only? (Asking questions)*
3. *Do you believe we should preserve history? Explain. (Text to self connection)*
4. *What do you think would have happened if the Chinese refused to build the wall? (Asking questions)*
5. *What words did the author use to help you visualize how the wall was created? (Visualize)*

Extension Activity

While the Great Wall was meant to keep invaders out of China, the Silk Road was letting people in. Both have many differences but are also similar. Research the Silk Road and create a travel brochure. Highlight the history, important stops that offered services to travelers, and the contributions it made. Share your brochure with your teacher, classmates, or family.

Table of Contents

A Giant Dragon

For thousands of years, the Great Wall of China has stretched across China's northern **provinces**. It winds like a giant, sleeping dragon from the Pacific coast in the east to the Gobi Desert in the west. It reaches across plains, mountains, and sandy deserts. It is the longest manmade structure in human history.

Did You Know?

The Great Wall of China is about 5,500 miles (8,851.8 kilometers) long.

The Great Wall has been extended, modified, and repaired over the centuries.

The Great Wall of China was originally built to protect Ancient China from invaders. The wall itself is not a single structure. Instead, it is a series of walls and **fortifications**. Over many centuries, sections of the wall were built and rebuilt by different Chinese emperors. Throughout China's history, more than 20 states and dynasties have worked on the wall. The most famous sections are those built by the Qin **dynasty** (221 BCE- 206 BCE), the Han dynasty (206 BCE – 220 CE), and the Ming dynasty (1368 – 1644).

The Great Wall of China stretches across northern China and has become one of the world's most famous landmarks.

Thousands of workers carry materials by hand to build sections of the Great Wall.

Building the Great Wall was a massive undertaking. Many people and materials were needed to build this enormous structure. Workers built the Great Wall without sophisticated equipment or machines. They did not have electrical power or motors. Instead, people worked side-by-side to build the wall by hand. The work was hard and many workers died during the Great Wall's construction.

Although the Great Wall was designed to keep invaders out, it also helped to unify the Chinese people. It became a source of pride for China. Today, the Great Wall is a symbol of China's enduring strength and accomplishments.

China's First Walls

The Great Wall may be China's most famous wall, but it is not China's first. The Chinese people built many walls before it. These walls were often built for protection. In ancient times, some Chinese people lived as hunters and gatherers. They roamed the land and hunted wild animals for food and clothing. Others settled as farmers. They tamed animals and planted crops. Groups of farmers formed small villages. These farming villages harvested food each season. They stored excess food and supplies until the next planting season.

As people learned about the villages' food stores, the residents faced danger from attacks. **Nomadic** tribes **raided** villages to steal food and supplies. In order to protect themselves, many early Chinese farming villages built walls to keep out invaders.

This is a food container from the Western Zhou dynasty (1046-771 BCE), which ruled over most of central China.

Hangtu Building Method

Most early Chinese walls were built using a primitive construction method called hangtu. The word hangtu comes from the Chinese words hang, which means beaten, and tu, which means Earth. The hangtu method used packed dirt to build walls. Builders first constructed a frame of wood planks or bamboo. Then they loaded dirt into the forms and packed the dirt with a pounding tool to remove any air pockets. This ensured the wall would not settle or sink. The workers slowly built the wall with many packed layers, each only a few inches thick. Once the wall reached the necessary height, the workers pulled away the wooden forms. A strong wall of tightly packed dirt remained.

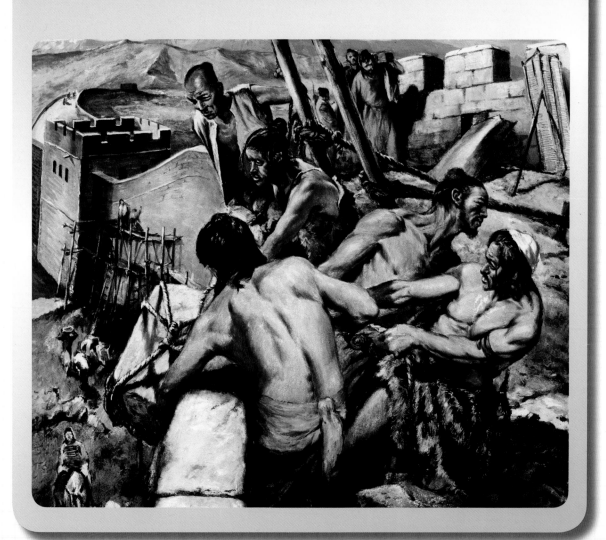

In Ancient China, the land was divided into seven states, each ruled by powerful nobles. These states frequently fought each other and northern **barbarians** for territory and power. This time was known as the Warring States Period (475 BCE – 221 BCE). During these years, the rulers built walls across China to define and protect their territories. The walls surrounded entire states and stretched for hundreds of miles.

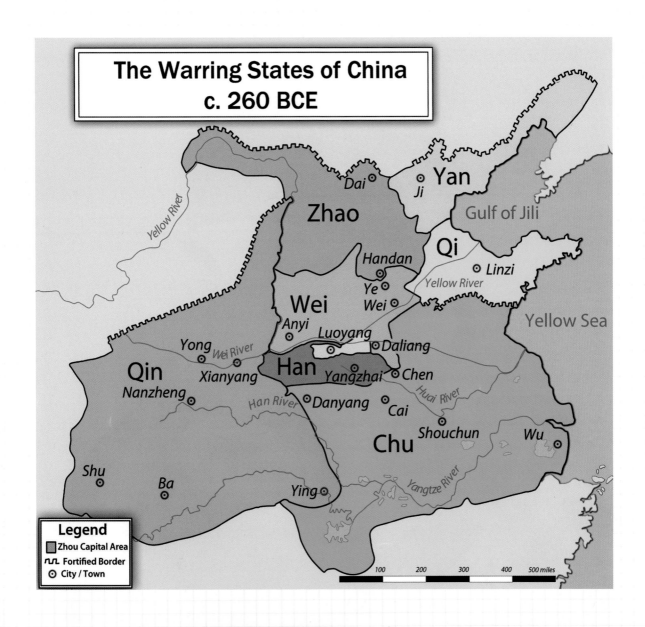

Near the end of the Warring States Period, the Qin state emerged as the most powerful in China. By 312 BCE, Qin fought to control all of China. In 246 BCE, a 14-year-old boy named Zheng became the king of Qin. He was a fierce and ruthless fighter. By 221 BCE, Qin defeated all the Chinese states. Zheng became the first **emperor** of China. He called himself Qin Shi Huangdi.

A terracotta warrior stands along the Great Wall. China's first emperor, Qin Shi Huangdi, ordered the construction of both.

Qin Shi Huangdi wanted to remain the emperor of China. He knew he needed to defend China from invaders. At the time, barbarians to the north were China's greatest threat. Some walls already existed in the northern provinces. Qin Shi Huangdi ordered the walls in the north to be linked together. They would form one great wall to keep out invaders.

These sections of the Great Wall were built during the Qin dynasty.

The Wall of Qin

Qin Shi Huangdi wanted his wall to be longer than any other in China. He demanded a 10,000 li wall. A li is a Chinese measurement that is about 1,760 feet (536 meters).

Did You Know?

A 10,000 li wall is long enough to stretch from Boston to San Francisco.

Qin Shi Huangdi's wall would also be more complex than previous Chinese walls. He planned for the Wall of Qin to be a series of towers linked together by sections of wall.

At this time, there were no machines that could be used to construct this massive project. Instead, millions of workers built the wall by hand. Most of China's men were ordered into service. Slaves, peasants, farmers, intellectuals, and criminals alike were forced to build the wall.

Sections of the Great Wall built during the Qin dynasty have deteriorated.

Qin Shi Huangdi appointed his trusted general, Meng Tian, to supervise the wall's construction. The general organized supply bases across China along the wall's path. After supplies arrived at the bases, construction began. First, workers built watchtowers and **garrison** towers. Massive brick and stone garrison towers were built every few miles. They held hundreds of guards in case of an attack. Between the garrison towers, the workers also built tall watchtowers. The watchtowers were spaced every few hundred yards. Archers atop these towers could shoot any attacker.

Sections of wall connected the towers. The walls' height varied depending on location. In flat areas and sections with military importance, the wall was built higher. In steep mountains, the wall was built lower. In general, the wall was about 23 to 26 feet (7 to 8 meters) tall. The wall's base measured about 7.1 yards (6.5 meters) wide. Its top measured an average of 6.3 yards (5.7 meters) wide. It was wide enough for troops to march across it.

The beacon tower of the Han dynasty rises above the wall at Dundun Mountain in Dunhuang County, Gansu.

Brain Builder!

Beacon towers were used for passing military messages. They were often built on the tops of the mountains to watch the movements of enemies.

To build the wall, workers used the hangtu construction method and local materials. In mountain regions, they packed stone and brick with the dirt. In desert areas, they mixed sand with debris and wood to build the wall.

Sections of the Great Wall were built using the rammed earth or hangtu method, which tightly packs layers of dirt into wooden frames to form walls.

Qin Shi Huangdi

Qin Shi Huangdi, China's first emperor, had a lasting effect on China. He united separate states into a unified China. He standardized China's currency, writing, weights, and measures. He was responsible for roads and canals built throughout the nation. He also ordered the construction of the Great Wall of China. Although he improved China in many ways, Emperor Qin was also a harsh leader. He ruled with strict laws and severe punishments. He outlawed most forms of religion and burned many books. After his death, Emperor Qin was buried with an army of life-size clay soldiers to guard him in the afterlife.

Under the supervision of soldiers, workers haul heavy building materials on their backs to build the Great Wall.

The life of a wall worker was difficult. They worked long hours, from sun-up to sundown. Soldiers guarded them as they worked. The workers lived in camps next to the wall. The housing was poorly constructed and provided little shelter from the weather. The workers did not have blankets or beds. Many of the men slept outside on the ground.

Workers often had little to eat. Food supplies were limited in China because many farmers were taken from their fields to build the wall. In addition, bandits often stole the food sent to workers. The scarce food supply and limited shelter contributed to many deaths.

The Great Wall has been called "the longest cemetery on Earth" because many workers died while building the wall. Many of these workers are buried underneath sections of the wall.

The Wall of Qin took about nine years to build. When complete, the wall stretched about 3,106 miles (5,000 kilometers) from Lintao in the west to Liaodong in the east. It served as a defensive structure in the north. It also symbolized the emperor's power.

Brain Builder!

Most parts of the Great Wall were built along the mountain ridge, because the mountains increased the wall's defensive position.

The Wall of Qin stretches across northern China, connecting smaller walls into one Great Wall to defend China's northern provinces.

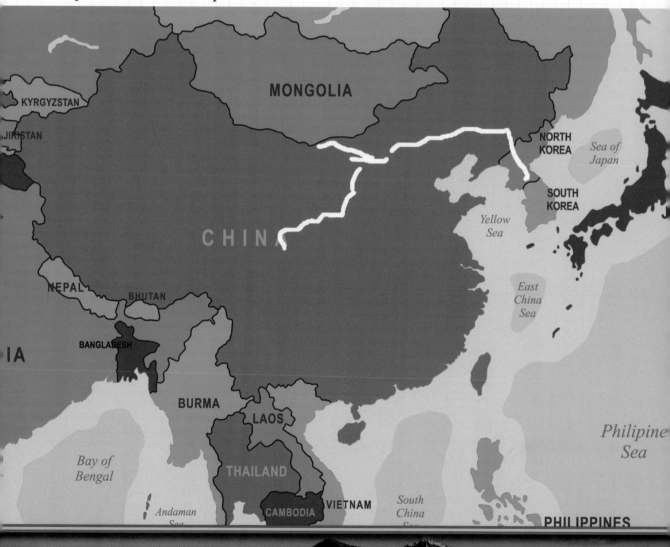

Sections of wall connect towers on the Wall of Qin.

The design and layout of the Wall of Qin was followed by future Chinese emperors. When they rebuilt a section of the wall or added new ones, they followed Qin's original structure. The Wall of Qin became the basis of the Great Wall of China.

Some sections of the Great Wall are likely to disappear in 20 years because of natural erosion and human activity, experts say.

Prosperity and Expansion

For most of China's history, walls such as the Great Wall were used for defense. Walls blocked invaders. They separated fighting Chinese states. During the Han dynasty, however, the Great Wall was used for a new purpose: trade.

Did You Know?

The Great Wall reached its longest length during the Han dynasty.

The Han dynasty ruled China from about 206 BCE until 220 CE. Han emperors restored peace and prosperity to China. Arts, literature, and inventions thrived during this period. For many years, work on the Great Wall stopped. No new sections were added. Many existing parts of the Great Wall fell into disrepair.

By the time of the sixth Han emperor, Wu Di (156 BCE-87 BCE), the northern tribe of Huns had become powerful. Wu Di ordered the construction of more walls to protect China's northern borders. He extended the Great Wall by about 300 miles (482 kilometers) to the west. He also added a chain of watchtowers beyond the wall's end. These watchtowers served as an early warning system. Soldiers manning the towers could signal to the next tower in an attack. The message could travel back to the main garrison and troops.

Builders often used local materials to build sections of the Great Wall. This section of the wall, built during the Han dynasty, is constructed from local plants and soil.

Over time, erosion has worn down parts of the Great Wall built during the Han dynasty.

Wu Di's wall ran across the western desert. In this region, there was very little dirt, stone, or wood available for construction. Instead, workers used local sand, branches, and **reeds**. Workers placed layers of reeds in several sections of the wall to give it additional strength. They layered the sand and reeds one on top of another. They pounded each layer down. On average, each layer measured about 4.7 to 5.9 inches (12 to 15 centimeters). The resulting wall was as hard as concrete.

Emperor Wu Di also ordered the construction of several important passes. Passes are massive defense structures on the wall, usually located in places of military importance. They often include square walls, gate towers, and moats. In the west, the Yumenguan Pass and the Yangguan Pass were built. In the north, the Yanmenguan Pass and the Niangziguan Pass were built. The passes controlled entry and exit through the wall.

Hundreds of thousands of men and women carried supplies on their backs. Sometimes, the workers formed a line and passed materials from person to person. Workers also pushed small handcarts to carry stones. They used tools such as levers, ropes, and cranks to raise and lower materials. Donkeys and goats helped carry loads of materials.

The Yangguan Pass was a vital part of the Silk Road, an important trade route between China and the Mediterranean.

The Silk Road runs from Xian to Dunhuang, where it divides into the Southern Route, Central Route, and Northern Route.

After conquering the Huns in the north, Wu Di established peace with northern nomadic tribes and encouraged trade with foreigners. The Chinese traded silk, paper, tea, spices, jade, and other luxuries with people from the west.

In the shadow of the Great Wall, a trade route emerged. This route became known as the Silk Road. The Silk Road followed the Great Wall because it was one of the safest ways to travel. Bandits and nomadic tribes still roamed the land. Soldiers manned the length of the Great Wall to protect China from invasion. The soldiers also protected travelers and traders from attack.

After the fall of the Han dynasty in about 220 CE, a series of **frontier** tribes seized control of northern China. Several of these dynasties repaired sections of the wall and built extensions. Most of these projects were meant to keep other northern tribes from attacking. The time of peace and prosperity along the Great Wall had ended.

With the rise of the Tang dynasty (618-907 CE), the Great Wall's importance decreased. The Tang dynasty valued an offensive military strategy. As a result, the Great Wall was abandoned. Several centuries passed before the Great Wall regained its place in China.

The Great Wall, built over a period of 2,000 years, is the world's longest construction project.

Ming Dynasty Rebuilds

When the Ming Dynasty (1368-1644) rose to power, the Great Wall had lost much of its importance. Much of its length had fallen into disrepair. Guard towers sat crumbling and abandoned. Attacks by northern barbarian tribes left gaps in many sections of the wall.

The rulers of the Ming dynasty helped the Great Wall regain its magnificent structure. Over a period of 200 years, Ming emperors restored the entire wall. They added to its length. They also fortified it more than any emperors in the past.

Workers designed a drainage system to protect the Great Wall from erosion caused by rain. They built barrel drains at intervals along the wall. The rainwater traveled through the barrel drains, which extended out from the wall by about one yard (.92 meters).

Much of the Great Wall that exists today was built during the Ming dynasty.

The Ming emperors wanted to free China from the threat of foreign invaders. In the years before the Ming, Mongol leader Genghis Khan and his son Kublai Khan ruled over China. After Kublai Khan's death in 1294, the Chinese regained control of China. The Ming rulers knew they needed to repair the wall to defend against Mongol invaders that still threatened northern China. They spared no expense in building, fortifying, and extending the Great Wall.

Barrel drains spaced along the Great Wall funnel rainwater to protect the wall from erosion.

The Ming Wall stretched from the Yalu River in Liaoning Province to the eastern bank of the Taolai River in Gansu Province. It was carefully designed to protect important areas. The Xuanfuzhen section of the Great Wall near the capital city of Beijing was built in a series of double lines. The inner and outer lines improved the wall's defensive strength.

The double lines of the wall near Beijing, China's capital city, protect important areas.

The Ming Wall also had six passes, or fortresses. Three inner passes and three outer passes controlled entry and exit into the areas. Each was secured by gates. The passes were heavily armed with soldiers and were considered critical to defending and protecting Beijing. The Ming also constructed watch towers, signal towers, fortresses, and observation posts along the wall. These structures reinforced the Great Wall's defenses.

Additions to the Great Wall built during the Ming dynasty improved its defensive strength.

Sections of the wall built during the Ming dynasty feature bricks baked in kilns near the wall.

During the Ming dynasty, some advancements improved the building process. Much of the Ming Wall was built using bricks, tiles, and lime. Bricks were formed onsite and baked in **kilns** built near the wall. Bricks were more convenient than dirt and stone because they were lighter and easier to carry. This made construction quicker. Bricks were also an ideal material because they were strong and resisted freezing and erosion. Builders created bricks in multiple shapes so that they could easily be placed in different positions. They used lime mortar mixed with sticky rice juice to cement the bricks in place.

Ming crews also used stone to build portions of the wall. Workers used stones cut in rectangular shapes to form the wall's **foundation**, inner and outer **brims**, and gateways. In some sections, they built entire wall sections from stone.

After decades of work, the Ming restored China's Great Wall as a symbol of China's power.

Defense against New Weapons

In earlier centuries, earthen and wood walls could defend against simple weapons such as swords, spears, and arrows. During the Ming dynasty, gunpowder emerged. Muskets and cannons appeared. Ming builders used bricks and stones to make the Great Wall stronger to defend against these new threats.

Cannon in the Simatai Great Wall of China, Beijing, China

The Great Wall of China Today

In 1912, China's last emperor gave up his throne. After several decades of struggle, the communist People's Republic of China formed in 1949. Many communist rulers believed that ancient monuments such as the Great Wall were painful reminders of the country's past. They believed that these monuments should be demolished. Under China's communist leader Mao Zedong, parts of

Chairman Mao Zedong (1893-1976)

the Great Wall and other Chinese **relics** were destroyed.

After years of neglect, the Great Wall of China again fell into disrepair. Exposure to natural elements and storms eroded sections of the wall, making it shorter and smaller. Many parts of the wall lie broken in remote grasslands and deserts. Other sections have disappeared completely.

Human activity also damaged the wall. Some people have taken pieces from it to use for construction materials.

Exposure to weather and human activities has crumbled many sections of the Great Wall.

After Mao Zedong's death in 1976, China's new leaders wanted to preserve China's culture. The Great Wall became a source of national pride. In the 1980s, the Chinese government began to restore and repair it. Today, several sections of the Great Wall of China are open to the public. It has become one of China's most popular tourist attractions. Thousands of Chinese and foreign tourists visit the wall each day.

Ruined sections of the Great Wall are tended to by workers.

Sections of the Great Wall frequently visited by tourists require regular repair and maintenance.

More than 10 million people visit the Great Wall each year.

World Heritage Site

In 1987, UNESCO designated the Great Wall of China as a World Heritage site. A World Heritage site is a place of special cultural or physical significance. These sites are to be protected for future generations to appreciate and enjoy.

Throughout its history, the Great Wall of China has served many roles. It defended and unified the Chinese people. It granted safe passage to traders and travelers. It also opened China to the world, attracting visitors from many countries.

The Great Wall of China has become an enduring symbol of China and its culture. With its mighty structure, the wall is one of the greatest engineering wonders created.

Timeline

5,000 BCE – Ancient Chinese people settle in farming villages and build walls to protect against raids.

475-221 BCE – The separate states of China battle during the Warring States Period.

221 BCE – Qin Shi Huangdi becomes China's first emperor. The Qin dynasty begins.

221 BCE – Construction of the Wall of Qin begins.

206 BCE – The Han dynasty begins. The Han rulers expand the Great Wall.

121-101 BCE – Han Emperor Wu Di extends the Great Wall into the western desert. The wall protects trade along the Silk Road.

220 CE – The Han dynasty ends.

1215 – Mongol leader Genghis Khan breaks through part of the Great Wall and becomes ruler of northern China.

1368 – The Ming dynasty comes to power and rules China. The Ming rulers make significant repairs and expansion to the Great Wall.

1912 – The last emperor of China steps down. The Republic of China is formed.

1949 – China becomes the People's Republic of China. Communist Mao Zedong comes to power.

1980s – Chinese leader Deng Xiaoping renews efforts to preserve the Great Wall.

2008 – China hosts the Summer Olympics and many foreigners visit the Great Wall.

Glossary

barbarians (bahr-BAIR-ee-uhnz): members of a tribal society thought to be uncivilized

brims (brimz): the upper edges

dynasty (dahy-NUH-stee): a sequence of rulers from the same family

emperor (EM-per-er): supreme ruler of an empire

fortifications (fawr-tuh-fi-KEY-shuhnz): military works constructed to strengthen or protect a position

foundation (foun-DEY-shuhn): the base of a wall usually made of masonry

frontier (fruhn-TEER): the land or territory that forms the farthest part of a country's settled or inhabited regions

garrison (gar-UH-suhn): a military post where troops are stationed

kilns (kilnz): furnaces or ovens used for burning, baking, or drying something, especially one for firing pottery or baking bricks

nomadic (noh-MAD-ik): relating to a tribe of people that moves from place to place, usually following a food supply

provinces (PROV-ins-is): parts of a country outside of the capital city

raided (REYD-ed): suddenly attacked or assaulted

reeds (reedz): the straight stalks of tall grasses

relics (REL-ikz): a surviving object from the past

Index

Show What You Know

1. Which emperor first started construction on the Great Wall of China?
2. What method of construction did workers use to build early Chinese walls?
3. What materials did workers use to build the Great Wall?
4. How was the Great Wall used for non-military purposes?
5. What factors, natural and manmade, have damaged the Great Wall over the years?

Websites to Visit

www.travelchinaguide.com/china_great_wall

www.history.com/topics/great-wall-of-china

http://travel.nationalgeographic.com/travel/countries/china-guide

About the Author

Carla Mooney has written many books for children and young adults. She lives in Pennsylvania with her husband and three children. She enjoys learning about world history and hopes to visit the Great Wall of China one day soon.

Meet The Author!
www.meetREMauthors.com

www.rourkeeducationalmedia.com

PHOTO CREDITS: Cover © TrashTheLens; title page © lapas77; page topper © Chen Hanquan/yesphoto@gmail.com; page 5, 39 © feiyuezhangjie; page 7 © Angus McBride/Look and Learn; page 9 © Mudong; page 11 © Editor at Large; page 12 © Neville Dear/Look and Learn; page 13 © Phig88; page 14 © unknown; page 15, 38 © Hung chung Chih; page 16, 17 © chuyu; page 19 © oceanfishing; page 20 atthameeni; page 21 © Neale Cousland; page 22 © Pat Nicolle/Look and Learn; page 23 © Eva Serrabassa Sito Garcia/caracterdesign.com; page 25 © yangphoto; page 26 caichuqing; page 27 © CIHASAKPRACHUM; page 28 © Robert_Ford; page 29 © suronin; page 30 © Rudra Marayan Mitra; page 31© stray_cat; page 33 © trekholidays; page 34 © fotohunter; page 36 © Rawpixel; page 37 © Pedro2009; page 40 © Athenar, Paul J Martin; page 41 © PEDRE; page 42 © lachria77

Edited by: Keli Sipperley

Cover and interior design by: Renee Brady

Library of Congress PCN Data

Great Wall of China / Carla Mooney
 (Engineering Wonders)
  ISBN 978-1-63430-418-4 (hard cover)
  ISBN 978-1-63430-518-1 (soft cover)
  ISBN 978-1-63430-609-6 (e-Book)
 Library of Congress Control Number: 2015931732

Also Available as:
ROURKE'S
e-Books

Printed in the United States of America, North Mankato, Minnesota